BINARY OPTIONS:

Steps by Steps Guide to making money

With Volatility Indices Trading

by

Richard Lee

LEGAL NOTICES

COPYRIGHT

All rights reserved. No part of this book may be reproduced in any form whatsoever, electronic or mechanical, including photocopying, recording, or by any informational storage or retrieval system or re-distributed without the express written permission of the author. This book cannot be sold under any circumstance; you have only personal rights to this book.

DISCLAIMER

By using the information in this book you agree that this is general education material and you will not hold anybody responsible for loss or damages resulting from the content provided here by the author

Please note that Binary trading and trading in other leveraged products involves a significant level of risk and is not suitable for all investors. Before undertaking any such transactions you should ensure that you fully understand the risks involved and seek independent advice if necessary. Any opinions, or other information contained in this book are provided for general educative purpose, and do not constitute investment advice.

Copyright © 2018 Richard Lee

All rights reserved.

TABLE OF CONTENTS

Introduction 4

CHAPTER ONE 5

Introduction to Binary Options Trading 5

CHAPTER TWO 8

How to Trade Rise/Fall 8

    Sniper Graphic Worm Strategy 8

CHAPTER THREE 13

How to Trade Touch/No Touch 13

    The Trading Platform 19

    Does Not Touch Trade Strategy 20

    BEAR MARKET 21

    The Keltner Channels Strategy 22

    How to Trade Keltner Channels 22

    The Upper Border Strategy 22

    The Middle Band Strategy 25

    Up/Down (Rise/Fall) Strategy 26

    Moving Average 50 Strategy (The Red Line) 28

    BULL MARKET 29

    Keltner Channel Strategy 29

    Moving Average 20 Strategy (The Black Line) 31

    Moving Average 50 Strategy (The Red Line) 32

    Money Management 34

CHAPTER FOUR 35

How to Trade Digits Matches 35
    Digits Matches Strategy 36
    Procedure 38
    The Secret Number 39
    Rules of Digits Matches Strategy 41
CHAPTER FIVE 43
Conclusion 43

Introduction

Thank you for purchasing this book. My ultimate aim of writing another book in the Teach Yourself Series is to help you trade and make money from Binary Options. You don't need to pay someone a huge amount before you can learn how to trade most especially Binary Options.

I am sharing with you here my wealth of experience and strategies in trading which I hope will also be of help to you.

Please note that as at the time of writing this book, some features in the binary platform might have been changed but the principles remain the same.

All you have to do is literally follow all the principle and strategy outlined in this book and you will be guaranteed to CONSISTENTLY have high winning ratio which translates to a very striking Return on Investment (ROI).

Have it mind that trading is not a get rich soon scheme. You can actually trade and make a living from it if you adhere to some certain rules and principles that guides it. I am sharing with you here several strategies that will help you to do that.

It is my hope that reading this book will not only translate to equipping you with knowledge but also help you to make money in your trading business.

I hope you will not only read but also applied the knowledge you have learnt in this book. It is then that your trading fortune will come.

I have great confidence that what you will learn, if implement will grant you access to the Binary Options cake.

Happy reading.

Richard Lee

CHAPTER ONE

Introduction to Binary Options Trading

Binary Options are also called all-or-nothing options. As a binary options trader, you have two positions to decide i.e. will the value of an asset go up or will it go down over a set period of time? Depending on trade outcome the payout is a predetermined percentage or nothing.

For Example, if a trader anticipates that the value of EURUSD will appreciate in a given period of time, and is correct, then he profits a fixed amount. If the value of EURUSD drops however, the trader loses the entire amount of the investment. It does not matter if the asset exceeds the original price by 1 point or 50 points, the payout is the same. Binary is simpler to trade compare to Forex. You don't need to know too much technical details to trade Binary Options unlike in Forex. Apart from that, Binary Options are shorter term, sometimes as quick as just 60 seconds, allowing for repeated trade and successes. Furthermore it enables investors to take advantage of both bull (upwards) and bear (downwards) market trends.

Trading itself is simple. Once you've opened your account, go to the trading platform. Select the asset you wish to trade, the expiry time, whether the value will go up (Call option) or down (Put option), and then enter the amount you wish to invest. You are in control of your investment at every stage. At the expiry time, the set payout will be automatically added to your account if you traded successfully, or the investment amount deducted if not.

While most brokers out there only provide traders options of trading in currency or commodities or stocks and indices, there is another side of Binary Options which binary.com offers his clients to make money. This is Volatility Index.

Volatility Index trading is an aspect of Binary Options trading being traded on [Binary.com platform.](#) It is more stable compare to currency and is not subject to news as most pairs do. Volatility Indices has many instruments to trade like Volatility 10 Index, Volatility 25 Index, Volatility 50 Index, Volatility 75 Index, Volatility 100 Index, and the Bear and Bull market. Please see picture below.

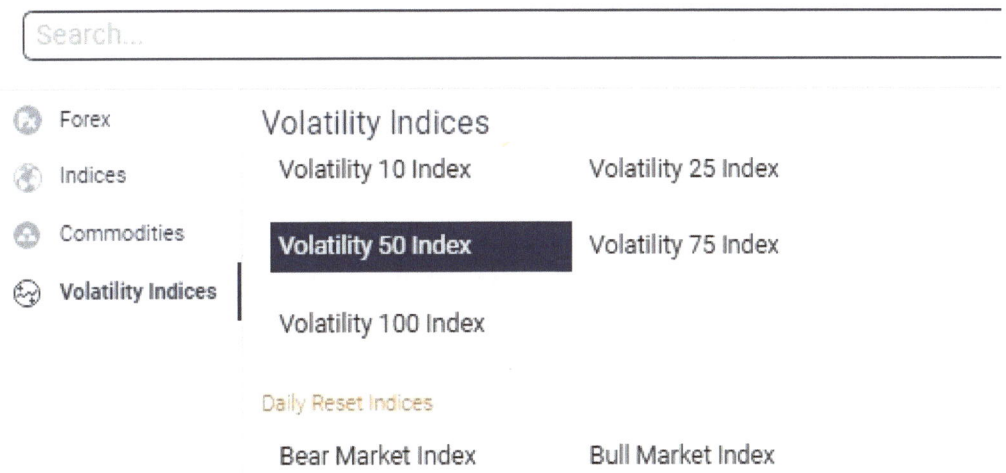

There are several options to trade under each Volatility Index. We have Up/Down (Rise/Fall, Higher/Lower) Touch/No Touch, In/Out, Digits, Asians and Lookbacks etc. See picture below,

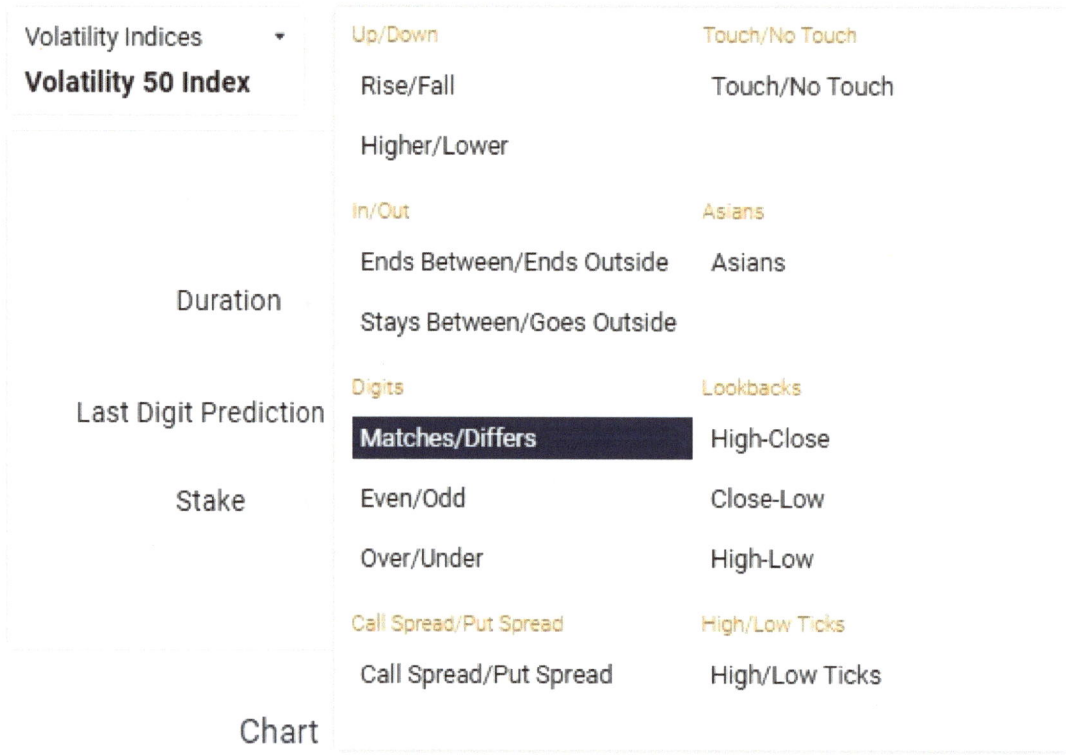

You may need to open each Index individually because you may not find Digit Matches in some like Bear and Bull market. All the same, is just to give you an idea of several trading options under Volatility Indices.

In this book, I will show you step by step how you can trade UP/Down (Rise/Fall), Digit Matches and Touch/No Touch.

CHAPTER TWO

How to Trade Rise/Fall

Sniper Graphic Worm Strategy

Let me explain how to trade Volatility Index with this strategy.

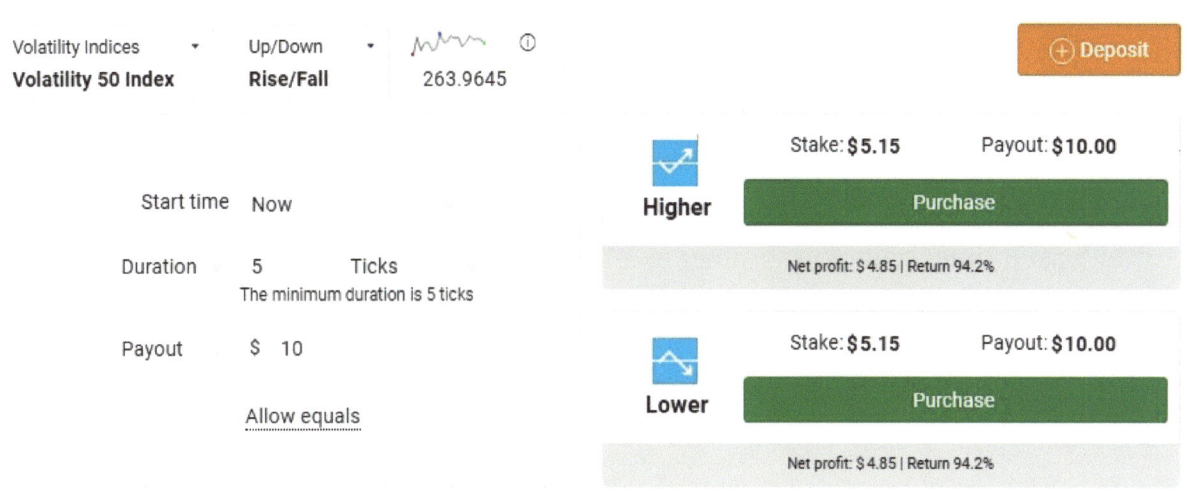

This is a Tick Strategy. Choose Up/Down and Rise/Fall. Under duration, you choose 5 ticks, set your stakes or investment amount and you can either purchase Higher or Lower.

In the picture above, can you see the line I pointed to with the Red arrow? That is the Graphic worm. It has four parts. The Red, Blue and Green small round part. The extreme end has the green round head like a worm. The fourth part is the colour display price 264.0470 as seen above. See picture below

The Red arrow points to the round part. The Blue arrow points to the round part and the Green arrow points to the worm head.

Rules of this Strategy

Our focus is the head of the Worm and the colour display price which must be BLUE or RED. **When the head of the worm changes to RED, counts the next successive head and colour display price.** If the next successive head and colour display price is also RED at least 3 times without any other colour in between, you must be ready to take your position(in this case HIGHER). Then when this occur, the next colour that comes up which is BLUE, immediately click on Higher.

BUT if the head of the worm is BLUE, counts the next successive number colour display price, if BLUE consecutively without any other colour intersperse in between. Then get ready to take your position which is LOWER. So in this case, immediately the next colour comes up which is RED, click on LOWER.

Please note, the colour display price or head of BLUE indicates UP or Higher while RED colour indicates Down or Lower

Let's see example,

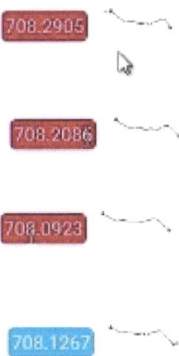

As you can see from the snapshot above.

The first colour display price was **RED** together with a graphic worm of **RED** head. The next immediate number colour was **RED** with **RED** head worm. This was followed immediately by another **RED** number colour with another worm with **RED** head.
Once you see three successive colour display price and head of the same colour without another number colour or head in between. Get ready to take your position.

Now, you can see that the fourth number was **BLUE** with a **GREEN** head. It doesn't matter. The sequence of number was met with the previous three **RED** numbers and head in sequence. Once this happen click on PURCHASE HIGHER.

And please note that immediately the colour display price changed to **BLUE**. You click on PURCHASE HIGHER simultaneously.

Let me show you another example.

BLUE heads come up with **BLUE** colour price! Count 1

The second price of the motion that comes up after that is still **BLUE**! Count 2

The third price of the motion that comes up after that is still **BLUE**! Count 3

Get ready to click **PURCHASE LOWER** after this. We already have three **BLUE** number and head in sequence that was not affected by another number colour.

And the color display price is still **BLUE,** is still okay. No problem.

After this, the color display price changes to **RED**, then immediately click **PURCHASE LOWER**.

Let me show you another example,

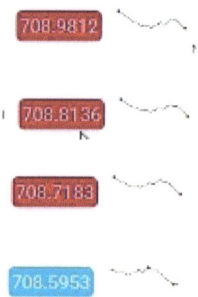

RED heads come up with **RED** colour price! Count 1

The second price of the motion that comes up after that is still **RED**! Count 2

The third price of the motion that comes up after that is still **RED**! Count 3

Get ready to click **PURCHASE HIGHER** position after this. We already have three **RED** number and head in sequence that was not affected by another number colour.

After this, the color display price changes to **BLUE**, then immediately click **PURCHASE HIGHER**.

But for instance if **RED** head appears, and I start to count from the first **RED** head, if the colour price and head is not in SEQUENCE(Disorganized), then the count will be invalid. I will disregard that and look for another better sequence.

Money Management

This strategy works and it will help you to make money from Volatility Binary Options easily than in currency. However, there is no strategy that is 100% perfect. If a strategy helps you to win 6 or 7 out of 10 trades. It is a good strategy.

The other key aspect of trading is Money Management. In case of losses, you must be ready to use Martingale Strategy to recoup your losses.
Below is a format of a sample MATINGALE you can used to recover your capital.
$0.5, $2.5, $6.25, $15.63, $39.07, $97.66.
What this mean is that if you stake $0.5 and you lose, in the next trade input $2.5, if it results into losses, in the next trade again put $6.25 and so on in that order… By doing this, you will be able to recover your losses and still be in profit after each trades.

Please note that the stake is depending on your capital. You can as well develop your own money management style depending on your capital.

CHAPTER THREE

How to Trade Touch/No Touch

To trade Touch/No Touch you will need Trading View Platform to get the chart.

There are two ways to get your Trading View Binary Platform.

(1.)   You can either go straight to https://tradingview.binary.com/v1.3.11/main.html or

(2.)   You go to binary.com on your browser and follow the steps below

Click on Platforms as shown below

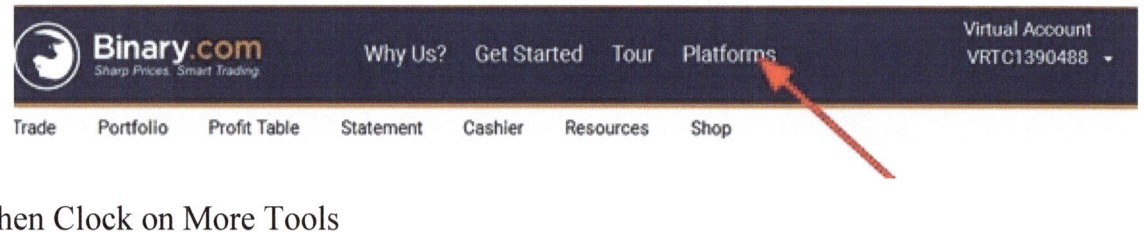

Then Clock on More Tools

Then Click on Try Trading View as shown below

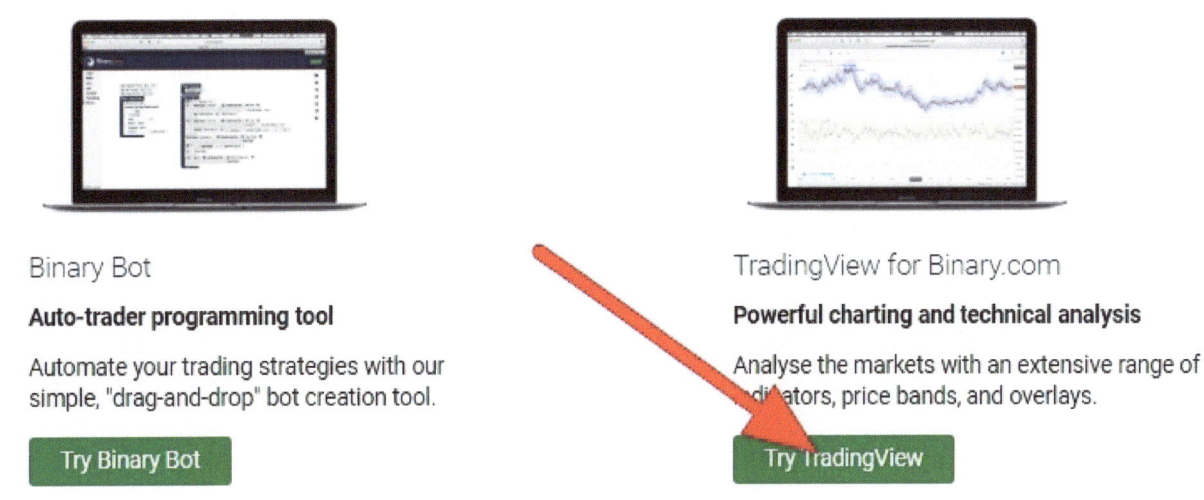

The Chart Will Load like this

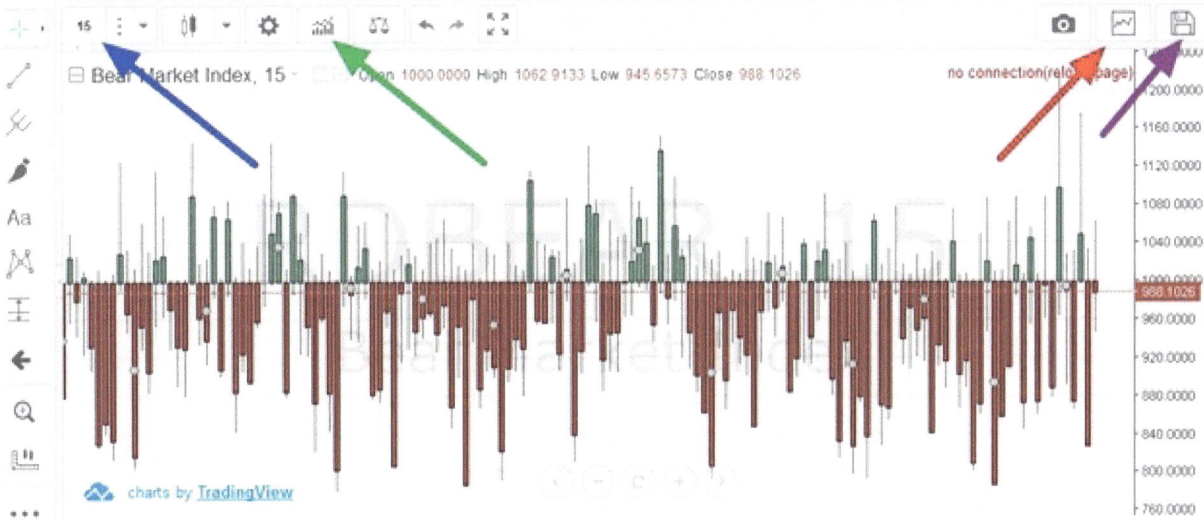

The Red Arrow indicates where to get the Instrument to Trade. When you click on it, it will bring a page like this shown below and you can choose Bear or Bull Market.

The Green Arrow is where to choose the Indicators.

The Blue Arrow is where to choose the Time Frame which could be 15mins to hrs. And the Purple Arrow is where to save the settings so you can see it when next you come back to trade.

See sample snapshot below

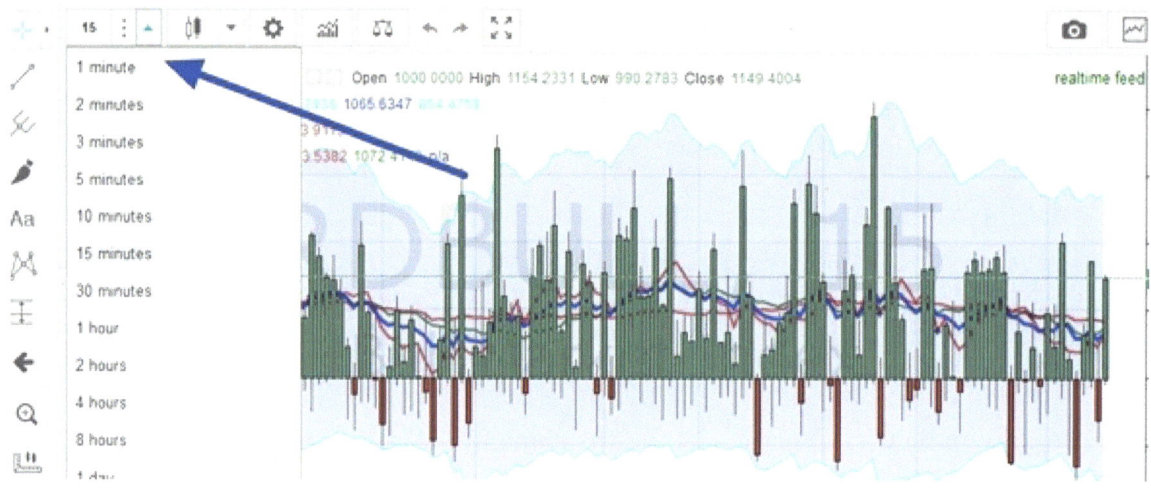

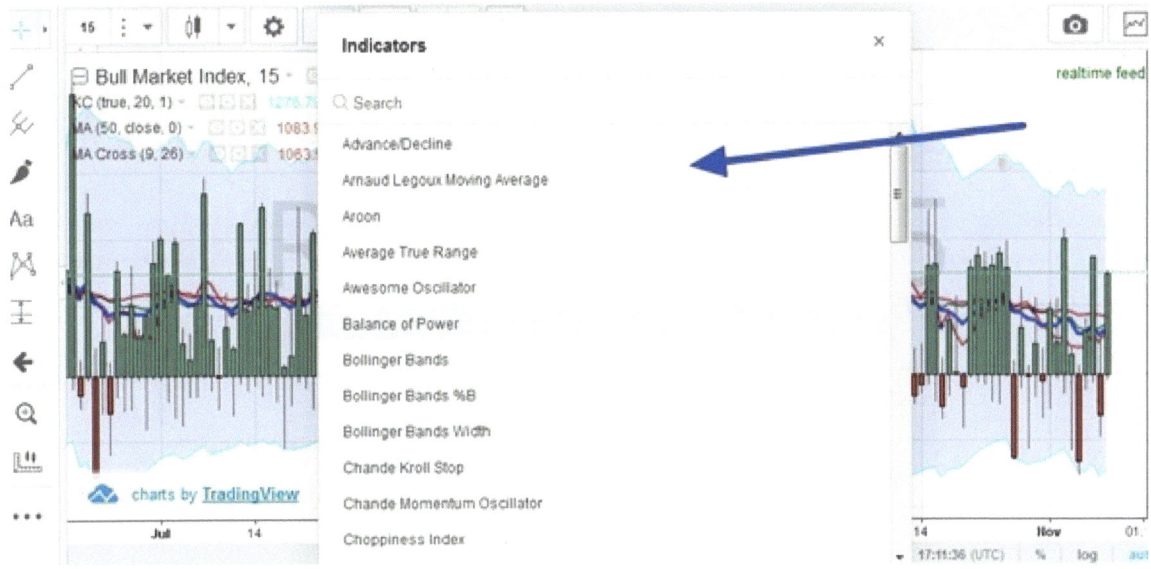

Once your chart is loaded. You will now configure your charts with two Indicators for our strategy.

The first is the Moving Average and the second is the Keltner Channel.

For Moving Average Settings

Choose Moving Average in the indicators and fill the details as shown below.

We are going to make use of Moving Average 20 and Moving Average 50.

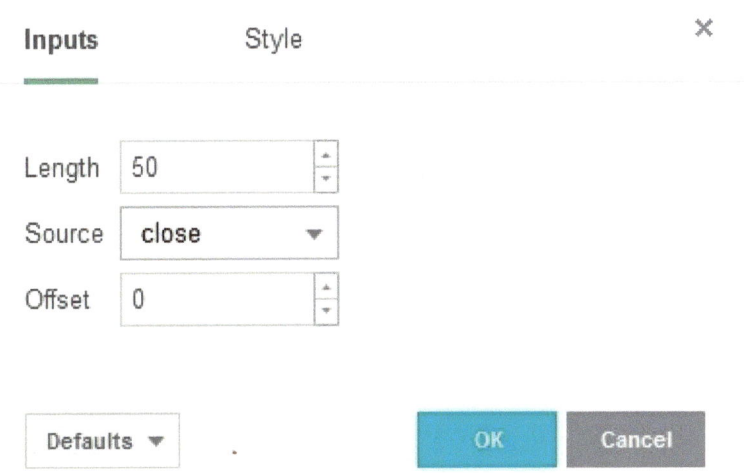

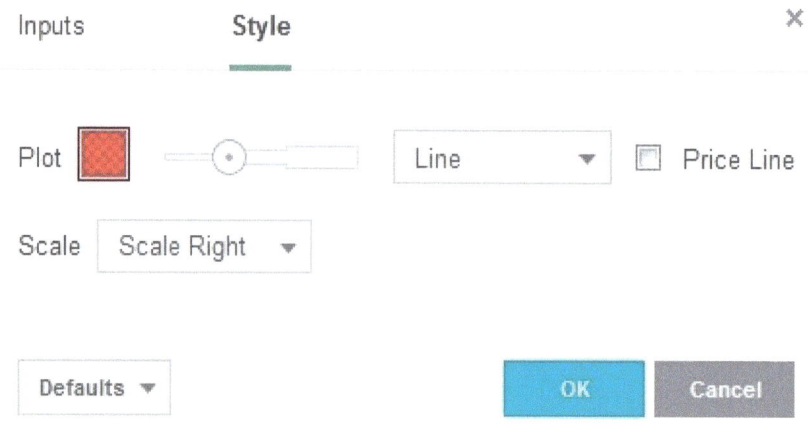

We are using Red Colour for Moving Average 50. Once this is done. Add Moving Average 20 too. You can choose any colour of your choice. Click Ok. And it will be inserted to your chart.

For Keltner Channel Settings

Choose Keltner under the Indicator list and fill the details as shown below. We are using 20 under the length as shown below. Please take note.

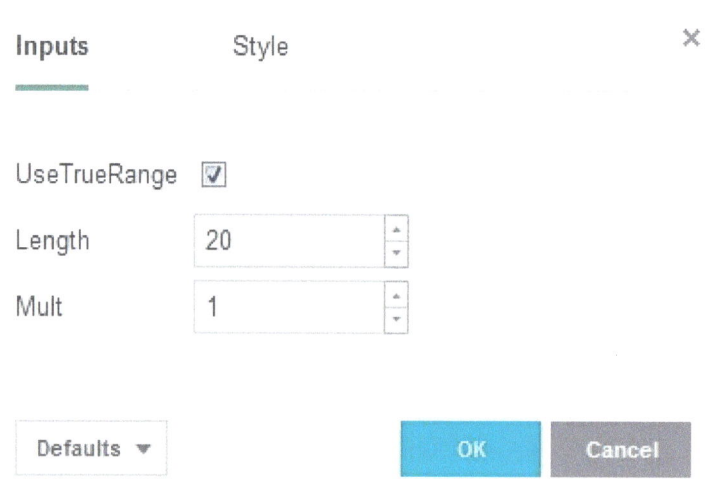

You can click on Style to change the colour of the lines. Kelter works like a Bollinger Band which has three lines. Each of these lines can be given different colour depending on your preference.

See below

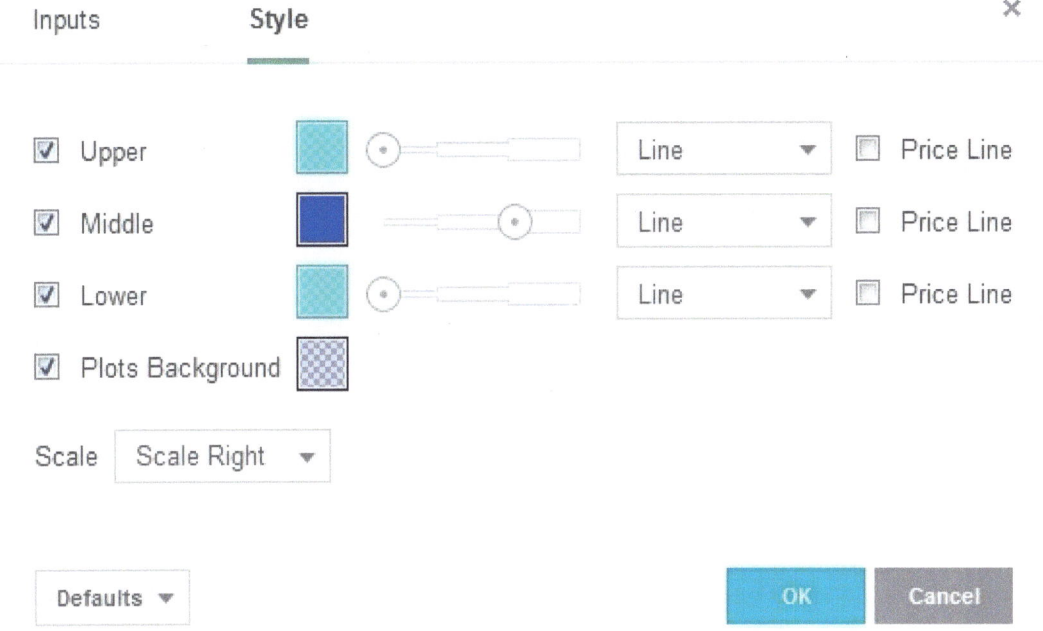

Then Click on SAVE to save the settings as template which you can open later when you come online to trade.

Now change your timeframe to 15mins or 30mins or 60mins. This will change your default chart where you have histogram to a chart like this below

The Trading Platform

Let's talk about the trading platform

Click on Volatility Indices. Choose Bear or Bull Market.

Then change from Rise/Fall to Touch/No Touch

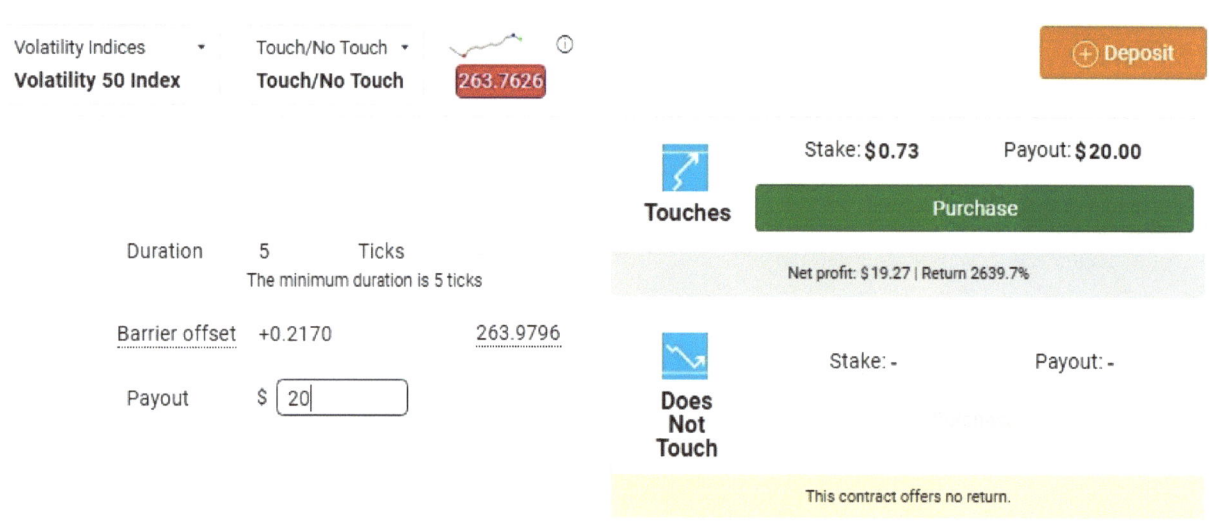

Duration: Is the time period you anticipate your trade will last or want your trade to run. It can be from 1mins minimum timeframe to 15hrs

Barrier Offset: Is like your Stop Loss in Forex. This broker will always give you a default barrier. In most cases, this barrier is very close to your entry. All you have to do is to change it to your own barrier.

When you change your barrier, you will also notice that your stake will increase while your payout will decrease or vice versa. Default barrier always give you an enormous payout with a very low stake. But once you reduce the barrier your stake will increase and payout will decrease

Touches: In this case, you are predicting that the market will touch a determine price level during a period of time.

Does Not Touch: In this trade, you are predicting that the market will not touch your barrier (price level) during a given period of time.

Let's look at how to trade Does Not Touch using Moving Average and Keltner Channel Strategy.

Does Not Touch Trade Strategy

In this section, I will show you how to trade Does Not Touch using Keltner channels. However, please note that you can apply the principle behind this strategy to trade UP/DOWN (Rise/Fall) too. Don't restrict yourself to Does Not Touch. You can use it to trade Rise/Fall as well. The reason why I am teaching you Does Not Touch is because if you get it right, you can easily make more money with it as it offers you a higher Returns on investment like 300% and above compare to Rise/Fall that offers you 30, 35% atimes or even less.

BEAR MARKET

The nature of Bear Market is to open high and trade lower. This means it will or always open above the closing price of the previous day, rally to reach a high then falls for the rest of the day. This nature gives us an edge to know the Trend of this market, which is always bearish.

As you can see from the chart above, the market opens high above the previous day close (starting from 00GMT), traded higher and fell for the rest of the day. You can check the chart to confirm this. Please check the Red Arrow. It is use to depict where the market opens and how it rally to the day's high before it fell.

When trading Bear market, we are taking our trade signals based on the bearish candle only.

In this case, we are trading in line with the trend- Being a bear market. Like we already know in Forex, the trend is your friend. Don't trade against the trend.

The Keltner Channels Strategy

The settings must be set to 20, 1 as shown above in the previous page.

There are two ways you can trade this strategy. It can either be for short or long duration.

For Short Duration Trade

In this case, you will use 15mins or 30mins time frame (chart) to get your signal. The expiry time (which is your duration) can be set as 30mins or 60mins depending on you.

For Long Duration Trade

You will set your duration as 4hours, 5hours etc.

How to Trade Keltner Channels

There are two ways to trade Keltner Channels.
  (1) You can trade candles coming from outside of the upper border of the Keltner Channels and closing below the upper border line or on it.
  (2) You can also trade the middle band of the Keltner Channels

The Upper Border Strategy

When the bearish candle coming from the outside of the upper border of the Keltner Channels close inside the Keltner channels (close below the upper border line or on it). Then we expect that the candles or the trades will try and touch the middle band of the Keltner channels.

In that case we place out DOES NOT TOUCH Trade and set our barrier as +6 of the default value. If the default value is +2.453 we will change it to +6.453. Another

way to get the barrier is to place your cursor about 1 or 2 points above the signal candle. **The signal candle is the candle that cross or close below the upper border of the Keltner Channels. It is the candle that is giving us a clue or go ahead that yes, you can place your trade now.**

Please note that the barrier is like setting your stop loss in the forex market.

Please check the arrows in the chart below for the Sample Trades

Bear Market Chart

This Chart has only Keltner Channels Indicator

Another Sample Trades below

This Chart has all the 3 indicators displayed.

You can see from the above chart that the market or candles was coming from outside of the upper border (from the higher) and goes lower inside the Keltner channels.

If you observe the above charts carefully, you will notice my time frame is 1hr. I used this for instruction purpose only. Use 15 or 30mins chart for trading purpose.

And I want to add this, when a trade is trigger on your 30mins or 15mins chart, you can open your 5mins chart to pick your entry. This is because, there are times the market will retrace upward before it moves in your direction- which is to fall. And if the retracement is long, it might hit your barrier before it picks the desired direction. So sometimes is better to wait for retracement to end on your 5mins timeframe before you place your DOES NOT TOUCH trade. It this case, your trade will be safe and cut your losses short.

The Middle Band Strategy

In a Bear Market when the bearish candle close on the middle band Line or above it, the trade (i.e. the next and successive candles) will move downward. In this case, we place a DOES NOT TOUCH trade. And we will set our Barrier as +6 of the default value as explain above.

Let's see trade Examples

The middle band line is indicated by the Blue Line.

Up/Down (Rise/Fall) Strategy

Like I said before, we are using two Moving Average 20 and 50. In this book, Moving Average 20 is indicated with black colour while Moving Average 50 is in Red Colour.

In a Bear Market, whenever the candles close below the Moving Average 20 line, the market will fall for the rest of the day till market close. What this signify is that the trend has turn to bearish, and we expect the market to continue downward in line with the bearish nature of the Bear Market. The market always respect Moving Average 20 and once it cross it and close below, the nature of the market is that it will trend lower for the rest of the day.

In this strategy, you are not going to place DOES NOT TOUCH Trade. You will trade UP/DOWN (Rise/Fall) trade.

Duration: Set your duration to more than 5-6hrs depending on the time you spot your signal.

Let's see trade examples for Bear Market Chart

Moving Average 50 Strategy (The Red Line)

In a Bear Market, whenever the candles close on or below the Moving Average 50 line, the next candle or trade will move downward. The same principle we observed in Moving Average 20 also applies here. Any close below the Moving Average signify change of trend, and we are expected to trade in line with the trend. The market always respect Moving Average 50 too, and once the candle cross it and close below, the market will make attempt to continue its fall. Once your trade signal is trigger, place your Up/Down (Rise/Fall) Trade and set your duration.

The Blue Arrow is to indicate loss. If you are to trade that, I expect that it will be a loss as it didn't move in our intended direction as expected. But in all, you still make profit. From the chart, we have 5 wins and 2 losses.

BULL MARKET

The nature of Bull Market is to open low and trade high. So it is expected that whenever it opens, the price falls lower than the previous day's closing price and trade higher for the rest of the day.

Since we are trading DOES NOT Touch, you will set your barrier. In this case, since is a Bull Market. You will insert negative sign (-) either -6, -9, -15 etc into the default value you see on the trading platform and set your duration. E.g If the default value is 2.3456; you will change it to -6.3456. This means you are predicting that the market will not touch your barrier over your set duration.

Let's look at sample trades for each of the strategies as discussed above…

Keltner Channel Strategy

Since we are dealing with a Bull Market, we are looking at Bullish Candles coming from outside of the Keltner Channel, crossing the lower border of the Channel and close inside it.

See the Arrows below

You can see from the chart above that the trade was coming from outside (coming from the low of the day) cross the lower border, either close on the line or above the line and trend higher.

Once you see a signal like this, you place your DOES NOT TOUCH trade. Set your Barrier as negative of the default value and set your duration too.

Trading the Middle Line of Keltner Channels in a Bull Market

Whenever the bullish candles close on the middle line represented by Blue line or above it, it is always expected that it will continue to go higher or rally. Once this is spotted, you place your DOES NOT TOUCH trade.

See Arrows below for trade Samples

Bull Market Chart

Moving Average 20 Strategy (The Black Line)

In a Bull Market, whenever the candles close above the Moving Average 20 line, it means the trend has changed to Up trend, and you can now trade in line with the trend. In such a case, the market will continue to rally for the rest of the day. Its nature will be to trend higher till market close.

Please Note: In this case, we are trading Up or Down (Rise/Fall) for the rest of the day. Whenever the bullish candle cross Moving Average 20 line and close above it, that is all for the day. The Market will continue to trend higher till market close. Once you spot this, place your Up trade and set your duration for the remaining hours of the day.

Exit your trade when it has given you double of your stake or wait till close of the day if you are sure it will not reverse.

See trade samples below as indicated by the arrow

Please Note that for this strategy. You must use 1hr timeframe or chart to get your signal for trading.

Moving Average 50 Strategy (The Red Line)

The same principle goes for Bull Market. In a Bull Market, whenever the candles close above the Moving Average 50 line, the market will continue to rally. Once this happen place your Up/Down (Rise/Fall) trade and set your duration.

I show the Blue Arrow above to indicate if you had placed that trade, it would had led to a loss.

A Word of Caution

I will expect that you don't blindly place a trade. The first thing you are to do is to mark area of Support and Resistance on your chart. Hope you know what Support and Resistance mean? They are zones on the charts where price that is going up can meet resistance and stop his upward direction and change to downward direction (Resistance) or zones where the price that is falling hit the support and stop falling and start buying (Support).

Once you draw your Support and Resistance, I implore you to ignore any signal that ask you to place your Up/Higher trade around Resistance and your Down/Lower trade around Support. Those are danger zones which will not make your trade to give you profit.

Money Management

Please make use of Martingale Strategy to recoup losses. That is the money management plan we are making use of to recover our loss trades and still be in profit.

CHAPTER FOUR

How to Trade Digits Matches

Under Digits match you are expected to predict the last digit of the Volatility Index price after 5-10 ticks. For example, you will win ten times your money if you predict that the last digit of the fifth tick would be 9 and it is so. But, if you predict 9, and the outcome is 8, you will lose your investment. This seems to be the most difficult, right?

Don't worry, I will give you the step by step procedure on how to make money with Digit match.

I have shown the snapshot below.

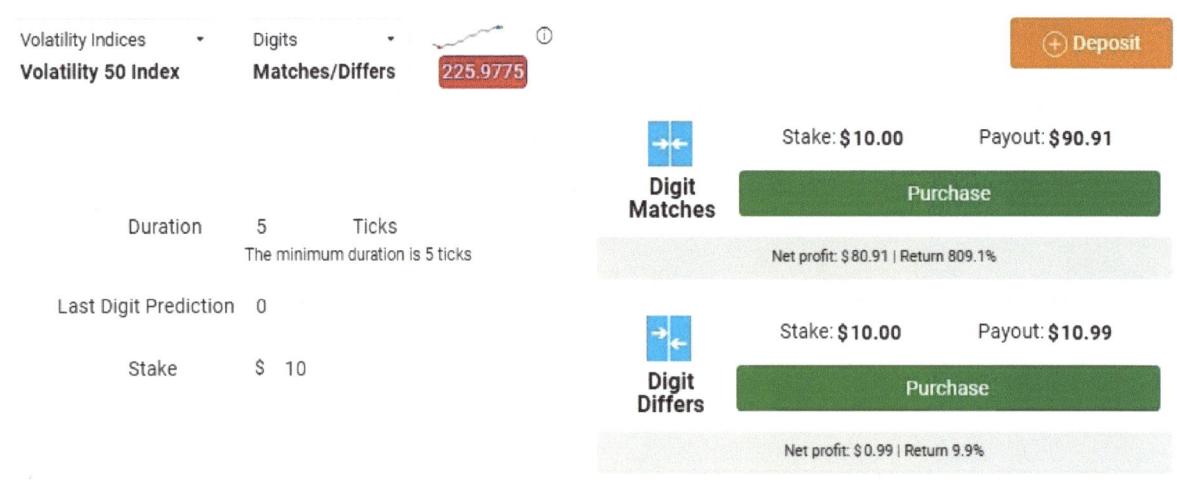

Once you click on Volatility Index of your choice, be it 10, 25, 50, 75 or 100. Change the UP/Down to Digits with Matches/Differs

Because it is very easy to predict Differs (predicting that the last digits of the 5th tick will not be a chosen number), the returns is very small.

To get the most out of this strategy, you will need at least $170 as capital to get started.

Digits Matches Strategy

Take a look at the table below. Do you understand what it means? I will explain each column for you.

Trials	Stake	Cost	Fixed	Returns
1	$1	$1	$10	$9
2	$1	$2	$10	$8
3	$1	$3	$10	$7
4	$1	$4	$10	$6
5	$1	$5	$10	$5
6	$1	$6	$10	$4
7	$1	$7	$10	$3
8	$1	$8	$10	$2
9	$1	$9	$10	$1
10	$2	$11	$20	$9
11	$2	$13	$20	$7
12	$2	$15	$20	$5
13	$2	$17	$20	$3
14	$3	$20	$30	$10
15	$3	$23	$30	$7

16	$3	$26	$30	$4
17	$4	$30	$40	$10
18	$4	$34	$40	$6
19	$4	$38	$40	$2
20	$5	$43	$50	$7
21	$5	$48	$50	$2
22	$7	$55	$70	$15
23	$7	$62	$70	$8
24	$7	$69	$70	$1
25	$9	$78	$90	$12
26	$9	$87	$90	$3
27	$12	$99	$120	$21
28	$12	$111	$120	$9
29	$13	$124	$130	$6
30	$15	$139	$150	$11

TRIALS

This is the amount of trials that will be made in which our hits or wins are expected to be made along the trials. Our $170 capital gives us the luxury of fumbling from trial one to trial thirty; along which we are expected to make a hit. The beauty here is that no matter where we make our hit, we shall always have a profit.

STAKE

Stake simply means the amount of money we are willing to invest or trade with. I guess you will understand better by merely looking through the table.

COST

This is the cumulative value of our stakes. By the time you will be taking your first trial, you will be paying $1. But by the time you will take your 11th trial, $15 would have been deducted from your account.

FIXED

The fixed here means the amount that we shall receive when we make a hit. Remember we are paid ten times of our stake. So, our FIXED at any point in time will be times ten of the stake at that particular point

RETURNS

This is our profit. It is calculated by subtracting the COST from the FIXED. That means that if we make a hit at the 12th trial; our cost there is $18. Because we stake $3 at the 12th trial, our fixed; which is 10 times our stake will be equal to $30. Therefore, our return at this point, being FIXED minus COST equals $30 minus $18, which gives $12. That means that our returns at that particular point will be $12.

Procedure

At digits matches, you are expected to predict from number 0 - 9, the number that will be the last decimal digit after the fifth tick. Once your prediction is right, you will get 10 times your stake.

We understand how this works already. You will input your stake, your prediction and click on Purchase Digit Matches.

Now take a look at that table up there again. Up there, there is "RETURNS" as a column. As I explained, it is our profit. HOW?

Like I said, we shall be predicting the last digit of the fifth tick. That means we shall have a probability of 1/10 (because we have ten numbers from 0-9) and as such, this seems very difficult. I am not saying I will give you a magic of knowing what the last digit will be out rightly. But, I shall be giving you a strategy which will ensure that you shall always be a winner even if you did not predict right several times. All that we are after is that we predict right just once in about 25 trials. This means that if we predict wrongly for 16 times and by the 17th prediction, we predict rightly, we will have a profit. What I am equipping you with is what is called a perfectly calculated risk. The only task you are shadowed with is choosing a number between 0 - 9. Every other thing will be taken care of.

The Secret Number

You know quite alright that we have to choose a number from 0-9 as our prediction that we hope to be the last digit after the fifth tick. Okay! Now, let me give you the secret number and the secret strategy. The numbers are 0, 1, 2, 3, 4, 5, 6, 7, 8, and 9. The ten of them of course. As you can see, all of them have equal probabilities. But sometimes I usually go for bigger numbers. (5, 6, 7, 8 or 9) with reasons unexplainable. Also, when going for these bigger numbers, I sometimes prefer even number among them (6 or 8).

On the contrary, if you do not have insight into any number at all and you want to really associate your choice number to something, then this may make a lot of sense to you. Look at this snapshot below

Click on Last Digit Stats as indicated with the BLUE arrow. This means statistics. If you click on it, it will bring a pie chart that will plot the frequency of appearance of each number from 0-9 for the set ticks you have chosen. You may decide to plot it for the past 100, 200, 300 past ticks. This will give you an insight to how often each number have appeared for the past ticks. Choose for the past 100 ticks if you must use the statistics because it gives recent information. Note that the number with the highest percentage is the number that had appeared most in the past 100 ticks.

NOTE:
The number we choose is in no way our strategy. The strategy lies in the tabulated formula. And note that WHICHEVER NUMBER YOU CHOOSE, YOU MUST NOT CHANGE IT UNTIL YOU HAVE WON. After you have won you may decide to use another number.

You must start all over again from the beginning once you win. (1st trial upwards)
For example if you choose **8**. On your 1st trial, it did not show (you lose your $1); 2nd trial, it did not show (you lose another $1, making $2); till the 7th trial (you lose another

$1, summing up to $7) and if by the 8th trial, you win, you will win $10. This minus the accumulated cost of $8 will leave you with $2 profit.

The point here is that you should not change the 8 (your prediction) until you have won. If you dare change it, you will lose your money. After making your hit, you may choose to change it or decide to continue with it. But, never change it at all when a game is still on without a winning yet. Once you do not change it, I am very confident that you will win before your 23rd trial. No matter how bad. And remember, no matter where you make your hit, you are sure of getting return. Just stick to the tabulated formula and let it be your guide.

Another note of warning is that **THIS STRATEGY CAN ONLY BE USED ONCE IN 3 MONTHS.** If you use it this month and intend to try it next month, it won't work. This may due to the fact that the broker watches our trades, and once they notice your sequence of wining, they will change the algorithm of the numbers. We don't want to play into their hands.

Rules of Digits Matches Strategy

- Open both the virtual account and the real account.
- Use the virtual account to try your hand with this strategy.
- Please make sure you practice with your Virtual account and build your confidence very well before going for Real account.
- As soon as you are ready for taking stakes, set all your parameters as instructed
- Make up your mind about the number you want to use
- Once you start, do not ever change your number, no matter how long it takes to make a hit; if you do, you will lose.
- Do not be hypertensive if you have not made a hit. It may come on the 24th trial or

even more.

- You must not relax in the middle of the stakes. Once the result is out for the 1st trial, feed the 2nd trial in immediately and so on, until you make your hit. This ensures that you do not make your trials independent but dependent on each other. This hastens your hit.
- **Based on our strategy, you are expected to make just 5 hits per day. This can be achieved under 15-20 minutes.**
- **With 5 hits per day, an average of $20/day is certain. That gives $100/week. This gives you target of $400/month.**
- Do not be greedy. If you choose to be, you are inviting trouble.
- Once the 5 hits has been made for the day, logout and calculate your profit for the day.
- If all these are strictly adhere to, your $400 is 100% guaranteed in month with this strategy alone.

CHAPTER FIVE

Conclusion

Let me rightly say the principles taught under Touch/No Touch can be used to trade Up/Down (Rise/Fall). Sometimes trading Does Not Touch could be very risky, in such a case, apply the strategy to trade Rise/Fall.

Keep to all the instructions in this book and you shall be amazed what your world will turn out to be. Do not be greedy and never be pessimistic. Also, do not be lazy. I believe this book is self-explanatory. Read carefully and be on the internet to practice all that was taught in it. With this guide I believe you can get started with your virtual account within 12hours of reading this guide.

I invite you to try my friend's Trend Trading strategies elaborated in his book [Binary Options: Steps by Steps Guide to Making Money from Binary Options Trading.](#)

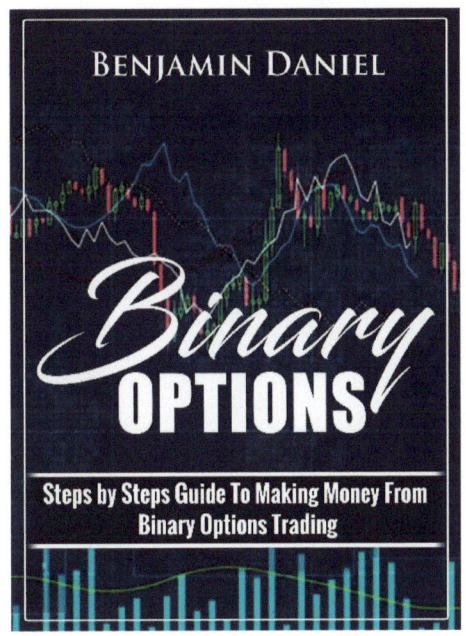

He discussed in detail about Trend- how to know the trend both manually and using indicators and how you can trade the retracement of any trend in Binary Options. The strategies outlined there can also be used to trade Volatility Indices for UP/Down (Rise/Fall) and Touch/No Touch. It is a very good book that will help you a lot.

****

Thanks for reading! If you enjoyed this book or found it useful I'd be very grateful if you'd post a short review on the site you purchase this book from. Your support really does make a difference and I read all the reviews personally so I can get your feedback and make this book even better.

"Thanks again for your support!"